DAVEY ALLISON
A Celebration of Life

BY LIZ ALLISON

FOREWORD BY BENNY PARSONS

This book is dedicated to my children, Robbie and Krista. I hope these pictures and words will allow you to always keep your Daddy alive in your hearts and your precious minds. You are both so special and I know God has many wonderful plans in store for you. May you hold a piece of your past with you, but never stop looking for the brightest star. One of God's greatest gifts is hope for the future.

SPECIAL THANKS

First and foremost, I want to thank the good Lord for being in my life and for giving me the strength, guidance, and the will to survive a horrible experience.

I especially want to thank my two beautiful children, Robbie and Krista, for putting up with Mommy while I was working on this book.

My thanks to Mom, Dad, Ma Ma, Grey, and the rest of my great family for their love, support, and understanding.

Thanks to all of Davey's family, especially Bobby, Judy, Grandma, Bonnie, and Carrie for sticking with me through thick and thin.

Thanks to all of my wonderful friends: Wayne Riner, Brett and Diane Bodine, Donnie and Donna Richeson, Terry and Lauri Smith, Max Easterwood, Donna Middlebrooks, Susan Bonnett, Mary Young, Dana Locker, Melissa Poling, Tammy Lampley, Georgia Mabry, Drinda Shipman, Jan Derrick, Darlene Hill, Shirley Salter, Regina Williford, Betty Ellison, Bill and Robin Heyne, Deani Joiner, and especially, Edith Bracknell, for truly knowing what friendship is all about.

A big thank-you to Mike Vaden, Brett Nelson, Ross Howell, Donnie Johnson, and Don Grassmann for helping to make this book happen.

Thanks to Benny Parsons for writing the book's foreword. Davey loved you and admired you. Your words are so meaningful to me.

A special thank-you to all of Davey's fans and the entire racing community for your undying love and support. I will always treasure Davey's racing days. Thanks for all the memories.

And lastly, I must thank Joe for carrying such a heavy load. Your patience, understanding, and support are truly a gift. You believed in me when I didn't believe in myself.

I only wish that I could thank everyone in Davey's and my life, but there are too many people to name. Please know that nothing is overlooked and that your support has brought Robbie, Krista, and me to where we are now.

Liz Allison

P.S. Thanks to Gucci and Lexi for all the kisses.

The author and publisher gratefully acknowledge the work of Don Grassmann, who contributed the photographs on the cover and in the pages of this book, except where otherwise noted. The book would not have been possible without Don Grassmann's cooperation.

Other photographs: page 4, page 11 (births of children), page 12 (hunting), pages 103-105, pages 112-113, page 117, page 119, collection of Liz Allison; page 7 (young Davey Allison), pages 10-11, pages 15-17, pages 18-19 and back cover, pages 20-31, collection of Bobby Allison.

Davey Allison racing statistics reprinted courtesy of Texaco/Havoline Racing, Bobby Allison Racing, and Donnie Johnson.

Designed by Lotta Helleberg.
Edited by Ross A. Howell, Jr. and Katherine A. Neale.

Library of Congress Catalog Card Number 95-78144
ISBN 1-57427-044-3

Printed in Hong Kong
Published by Howell Press, Inc., 1147 River Road, Suite 2, Charlottesville, Virginia 22901
Telephone (804) 977-4006

Fourth printing

HOWELL PRESS

CONTENTS

FOREWORD

The first time I laid eyes on Davey Allison he was wearing that famous smile that is now so familiar.

The first time I laid eyes on Davey Allison he was wearing that famous smile that is now so familiar. He also had a sparkle in his eyes that made you wonder what he had been up to. I now realize that sparkle was several things.

First, Davey was glad to be at a racetrack, to be around the things and the people that were so dear to him and his family. Second, he was around his heroes. Most people never get a chance to meet their heroes, but Davey was lucky: he could see a dozen in one weekend. Third, racing was how Davey wanted to spend his life. That came through loud and clear.

Davey could have chosen a much different, easier path than he did, and still ended up just as successful. His early days were difficult. He faced the same problems most young drivers face—a lot of late hours and never enough money.

I remember when, in the early '80s, Davey pulled his Saturday Night Special to Daytona to run some of the short tracks in the area after he finished fourth in one of the consolation races. I asked his dad if he shouldn't insist on Davey going to college and getting a degree to fall back on. After all, there was a chance that Davey wouldn't be able to make a living racing.

"No, I don't think that will work because racing is all Davey thinks about," Bobby said. "Davey also has great work habits and he understands a lot about a race. More than I did at his age."

Bobby was right. Davey didn't need to go to college. Auto racing gave him things a bachelor's degree never could have: fame, fortune, contentment, and pleasure. He was known worldwide and he made a lot of money. He was happy with his work, he could afford the toys he wanted, and he could give his family a nice home and whatever else they might need. And man, wasn't life fun! Can you imagine how much fun it was for Davey to follow his father across the finish line in the biggest stock car race of all—the Daytona 500! Wow! And, just a few years later, he won Daytona himself!

You, Davey Allison, you got a lot of pleasure out of life, but you gave a lot back to those around you. Your crews, the media, and—perhaps most of all—your fans enjoyed every minute they spent around you. You were great with the fans. I know you were tired, but you stayed, signing autographs until everyone was happy.

I miss that smile and that sparkle in your eyes, but if things work out right, I'll see them again. You'll say, "Come on, B.P., we got a 3/8 clay oval and it's more fun than Daytona!"

Benny Parsons
Charlotte, North Carolina

INTRODUCTION

Davey knew from a very young age that he wanted to race like his dad.

Putting together this book was a test for the old heart. There are so many things I want to tell everyone about Davey and what he meant to so many people. It is very hard to take somebody's life, and what they stood for, and put it on paper.

Davey experienced a lot in his life. Some of it was good and, inevitably, some of it was bad. But he had a positive attitude and he always used his bad experiences to his advantage by learning from the lessons they taught him.

Photograph for a local newspaper article about Bobby shows the Allison crew in 1968. Davey was seven years old.

One of the things I admired most about Davey was his drive to succeed. It didn't matter to him how large or small the task, he always gave it his best. He was a very determined person; once he set his mind on doing something, it was done right.

Davey knew from a very young age that he wanted to race like his dad. He started working at his dad's shop in Hueytown, Alabama. He began by sweeping floors and, eventually, he was driving cars.

I used to love to hear stories about his childhood and his early racing years. I especially loved stories about the Peach Fuzz Gang, which got its name because none of its members—except Grandpa, of course—shaved. They were a bunch of kids having fun. Those were great years for Davey. He loved Tommy, Mike, and Kenny Allison, Grandpa Allison, Greg Campbell, Randy Hill, and what they all accomplished.

I think a part of Davey wished for racing to stay the way it was in those times. But racing, like everything, continues to grow. The more money involved, the more people involved, and the more demands were put on his time. I think the Peach Fuzz Gang years and Davey's early years at Birmingham International Raceway helped mold him into the superstar that he was. When Davey made that big step to Winston Cup Racing, he felt that he was ready. His rookie title in 1987 and his two wins in his first year reinforced that feeling. He followed up his rookie year with two more wins in 1988, which meant the critics couldn't chalk up his success to beginner's luck.

Then, of course, came Bobby's wreck at Pocono, which ended his career as a driver. Davey was faced with losing his dad, his best friend, and his

Davey sits in the driver's seat of his dad's race car in 1973.

hero—all at once—as well as being burdened with the duties he assumed as the man of the family.

Those weeks following Bobby's wreck changed Davey's life forever. He was under a tremendous amount of pressure; he did not want to let down his friends, family, the race team, and his fans. I sometimes wonder how he kept going during this trying period. I believe it was his strong faith in God that carried him through those times.

The next few years would bring a lot of changes for Davey. Robert Yates bought the Texaco/Havoline team from Harry Ranier and the team was pretty much rebuilt from scratch. Bobby was eventually on the road to recovery, and several months later, Davey and I married and soon had our first child, Krista.

It was evident at that point that there was nothing greater in life to Davey Allison than his children. I still remember the look on his face when Krista was born and the tender way he held her in his arms for the first time. It was a powerful scene.

Then came little Robbie (Robert Grey), who is named after Bobby Allison and my father, Grey Mayson. Robbie was the first grandson on both

sides of the family. We were all so proud of him. Davey was so excited about having a boy to do things with. Thank God for us, Robbie is just like his Daddy.

Nineteen-ninety-two. What can I say about that year? Davey won the Daytona 500 at the beginning of the season and everyone's hopes were up for a championship year. This would be the first championship for the Davey Allison/Robert Yates team. Then in April, Davey's grandfather, Pop Allison, died after a lengthy illness. Pop's death shattered Davey's heart. He had spent much of his childhood with his grandpa. Despite the fact that

Probably Davey's happiest race memory was the historic 1988 Daytona 500, when he finished second to his father.

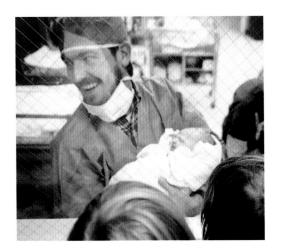

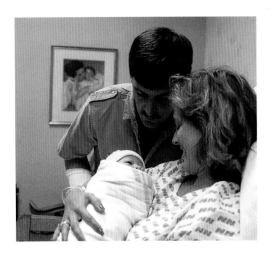

(Far left) The proud Daddy holds Krista, who was born on Christmas eve, 1989. (Left) We admire our beautiful baby boy. Robbie was born the day after the Talladega race, July 1991.

He loved racing, hunting, fishing, signing autographs for fans, and—first and foremost— Davey loved his family.

Davey was still grieving, he raced at North Wilkesboro two weeks after his grandpa's death. Davey was in a lot of physical pain from his wreck at Bristol the week before, but despite the physical and emotional pain, he went on to win the race, which he dedicated to Pop. The Victory Lane ceremony was bittersweet.

Then he headed to The Winston all-star race in Charlotte. After Davey took the checkered flag with Kyle Petty running second, the two crashed, leaving Davey injured again. He spent the night in the hospital, only to return to the track on Thursday and qualify for the Sunday race. At that point we were all reeling from the emotional roller coaster ride the family had been on. Little did we know, it was just the beginning.

July came and it was time to race at Pocono. After leading much of the race, Davey and Darrell Waltrip got together on the restart. Davey went for the ride of his life. He flipped eleven times before landing on the guardrail. He was airlifted to a nearby hospital as I, like so many others, watched from my living room.

Two things stand out in my memory of that day. One was Davey's brother Clifford and his wife Elisa showing up at my doorstep minutes after the wreck. The other was Larry McReynolds making repeated phone calls from the hospital to

An avid sportsman, Davey especially loved hunting.

keep me posted and calm me down. When we found out he was going to be okay, Davey's brother Clifford, my friend Donna, and I headed for Allentown in a chartered plane. When we arrived, I saw that big smile on his face and I knew he would be fine.

Davey had many surgeries and extensive physical therapy after this accident but recovered well. He returned home two days before the race at Talladega. Bobby Hillin was named the relief driver for Davey and did a great job. He was able to keep Davey leading in points for the championship.

Then, as if we hadn't experienced enough, on August 13, 1992, Clifford suffered a fatal crash at Michigan International Speedway. Davey and I were on our way to the Birmingham airport when we got the news that Clifford had passed away. The next few days were a living hell. After a lot of tears and prayers, Davey decided to race that Sunday. He knew Clifford would want him to go on.

Davey did go on, but he was never the same. Clifford's death changed everything about Davey. He was never able to get over the pain of losing his brother. In November, at the Atlanta race,

Determined to keep his points lead for the Winston Cup title, Davey was flown from a Pennsylvania hospital to Talladega four days after his 1992 life-threatening wreck at Pocono. He painfully practices getting in and out of the car, so that a relief driver can take over during the race that Sunday. Velcro was attached to his arm cast to help him hold the shifter.

Davey was leading the points for the championship—a championship he wanted to win for himself, for his grandpa, and for Clifford. He and Ernie Irvin got together, which took Davey out of contention for the championship. I have never seen a man handle so great a disappointment with so much dignity. Davey's concern at that point was for Ernie's safety. Davey would not leave the infield care center until he knew Ernie was okay. Alan Kulwicki went on to win the 1992 Winston Cup Stock Car Racing Championship.

This was very hard for me to take. I felt that Davey deserved the championship. He had conquered too much to get that close and not win. Davey always felt in his heart that everything happens for a reason and, five months later, I realized he was right. Alan Kulwicki was killed in an airplane crash on his way to a race in Bristol, Tennessee, in April 1993. We seemed to have a better understanding. Davey commented that he was glad Alan had won the championship, because Alan would have no more chances but, God willing, Davey would have many more.

Davey continued to amaze me with his strength and courage. He forged ahead, always looking for the best in everything. He spent all of his "down time" with his children and enjoyed our new home. He loved spending time with his family and playing with his dog, Hunter.

On Sunday, July 11, 1993, Davey raced at New Hampshire. In the post-race interview, Davey said hello to Robbie and Krista as we watched it from home. This would be Davey's last race.

On July 13, 1993, Davey died after the helicopter he was piloting crashed into the Talladega Superspeedway. I believe the world lost a great

person; I know that my children and I lost a devoted father and husband.

There is one thing I always tell my children and the fans I talk with to remember. Davey lived his life to the absolute fullest. He loved life and everything about it. He loved racing, hunting, fishing, signing autographs for fans, and—first and foremost—Davey loved his family. I think he should be an inspiration to us all. Robbie, Krista, and I have suffered a great loss, but we are thankful to have been such a big part of Davey's life.

I hope this book will help you see the side of Davey that those who were close to him saw: a man with an easy smile who looked for the good in everyone and in every situation, a person not without faults, but with the will to strive to overcome adversity, a man who loved and celebrated life and living. Enjoy.

Liz Allison

Nashville, Tennessee

The last picture the four of us had taken together at a racetrack was in the garage area before the start of the race at Pocono, June 1993—one month before Davey's fatal accident.

Early years

This is my favorite baby picture of Davey. He was only nine months old. What's especially funny about this photograph is that Davey hated to talk on the telephone.

*D*avey loved small children as a young person and always seemed to know how to entertain them, by rough-housing, tickling them, or being goofy. He liked most any kind of food that I fixed. His favorite was chocolate wafer cookies filled with cream, then frozen. He liked cream puffs and Swedish pan-cakes. At Christmas he always wanted me to make Swedish star rosette cookies—he was proud of his Swedish heritage (my side of the family).

Judy Allison

(Facing) Bobby and Judy pose for an Easter picture in front of their Crescent Drive home in Hueytown in 1966. Davey, age five, is standing in front of his dad. Bonnie stands in front of Judy, while Clifford has fun going through his Easter basket. (Left) Davey was lucky #11 with his seventh grade basketball team. He loved many different sports, but became more interested in baseball and football during his high school years. (Below, left) When he was seven years old, Davey made his First Communion at St. Aloysius Church. In the Catholic religion, Holy Communion is very important. This was a special day for Davey and the entire Allison family. (Below, right) Davey's sixth grade school picture from St. Aloysius Catholic school.

Davey listens in on Bobby's conversation about the performance of his car at Darlington International Raceway in 1975. The cast on Davey's arm resulted from flipping his go-cart while he was pretending to be a race car driver near his home in Hueytown.

(Facing) Davey stands with Erin Hogdon, the son of Warner Hodgon, one of Bobby's longtime friends, the night of Davey's very first feature event victory. (Above) Davey won driving a Chevrolet Nova at Birmingham International Raceway in April 1979. John Smith meets Davey with a cold drink and Bobby, as you can see, is very proud. (Left) Cousins Tommy (center) and Stevie Allison (right) congratulate Davey.

A father's thoughts about a son who was a special young man, to me and to a lot of other people—he was so focused that it could be aggravating at times. He had a younger brother who was also a very good young man, but he was just the opposite of Davey. I often use the following illustration to show their different personalities. Clifford could be guilty of some misdeed and he would turn on the charm to talk himself out of a whipping. Davey could be innocent of a wrongdoing, but he would talk himself into a whipping! Think of how determined he must have been! That same determination made him the great racer that he was.

Bobby Allison

(Above) The victory lap for Davey's April 1979 win. (Below, left) Davey and Bobby talk over qualifying. Neither looks too happy. (Below, right) Davey loved working on race cars as much as he loved driving them. He was one of the few Winston Cup drivers who could build a race car from the ground up.

(Left) One of Davey's first rides in 1979. He was attempting to qualify for an event at Birmingham International Raceway. His car is only primed, since he had no sponsor or decals. (Below) Davey had many wrecks at BIR. He was famous for his corner crashes.

(Right and below) Davey takes the checkered flag while racing in the Sportsman Division at Birmingham International Raceway.

(Above) Davey in 1982 at Pensacola Speedway. He spent a good bit of time at this track and at Birmingham International Raceway, running the feature events. (Right) At Daytona Speedway in 1984. Davey was running ARCA at the time. Later in the year he changed cars, driving the #23 Miller car.

(Left) Davey with his Lancaster Buick in 1986. (Below) At the Talladega Superspeedway in 1985, Davey was competing for the ARCA Championship, but he did not win.

Davey's second ARCA car at Atlanta Motor Speedway in November 1984. He went on to win this race.

(Above, left) Davey at a press conference at Talladega early in his career. Also pictured are Don Naman, Darrell Waltrip, and Dave Marcis. (Above, right) Davey holds the trophy for winning the 1984 Permatex 500 pole position. He also went on to win the race. (Right) In Victory Lane after winning the 1983 ARCA race at Talladega, Davey is joined by the UNOCAL RaceStoppers. His proud dad stands at the left of the picture.

(Left) Davey in Victory Lane at Atlanta. Holding the checkered flag are Grandma Allison, his mom, Judy, and Grandpa Allison. (Below) Davey could get pretty crazy in Victory Lane. At the 1990 Mello Yello 500 at Charlotte Motor Speedway, Davey sprayed everyone in range with his ice-cold Mello Yello.

Man of many faces

Davey was well known for his boyish personality. He loved to goof around and play jokes on people. Here's his expression after his qualifying effort left him in second place—definitely not where he wanted to be.

(Facing) In September 1992, Davey still wears an arm and wrist brace from his wreck at Pocono in July. (Above) Davey takes a look under his Busch Grand National car while Charlie Brock makes some adjustments. (Left) One thing I learned during our marriage was that Davey had become hard of hearing. It was kind of a joke around the house that he heard only what he wanted to hear. Race cars, of course, are very loud and over time, the noise can damage hearing. In this picture, one of Davey's crew members is trying to give him information on his car.

(Above) Davey runs to his car for the start of a race. (Right) Davey loved to watch other cars on the track. Here he's timing one of his competitors. (Facing) Davey helps his crew push his car out to pit road for qualifying. In the background is Sam Manze, our pilot and a longtime friend of the family.

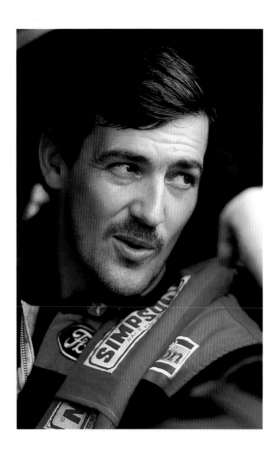

(Facing, above) Still strapped in his car, Davey discusses the outcome of a race with a crew member. (Facing, below) Davey loved his fans and always commented on how loyal they were. Many times after a race he would stand at the fence and sign autographs. (Above) Davey shares a laugh with his dear friend, Brett Bodine. They had a very special relationship, one that I know Davey treasured.

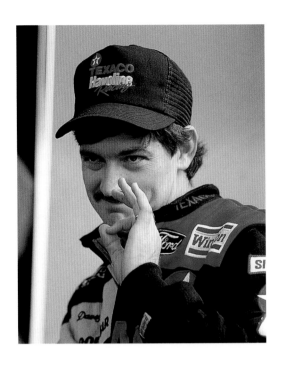

(Facing, above) That famous Allison grin. (Facing, below) Davey looks surprised at someone's qualifying speed. (Left, above) A big okay sign for his crew. (Left) This is one of my favorite pictures of Davey. He has just seen his mom and dad coming through the garage area.

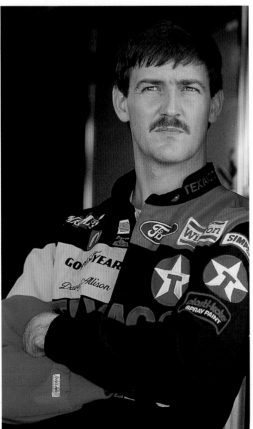

On Sunday mornings before the start of a race, Davey was very focused. He didn't talk much and was very serious.

(Above) Strapped in his car with the window net up, Davey is ready for the start of a race. You can see his intensity. (Right) This is his goofy "I'm thinking up a prank on someone" look. (Facing) Davey stands during the playing of the national anthem before the start of a Busch Grand National race.

(Facing) Davey sits on pit road waiting for the crew to give him word on his car, which had developed early engine problems. (Above) Davey and Larry McReynolds discuss a racing incident.

(Facing) The serious side of Davey. He looks as though something is weighing heavily on his mind. (Above) While this picture is very painful, it is a testament to the heart of Davey Allison. He was trying to make it through the weekend at Michigan after his brother Clifford died in 1992. During this quiet moment in his car, he uses a rag to wipe away his tears. (Left) Having just returned from Pocono after his horrible crash in July 1992, Davey discusses the game plan for the start of the Talladega race with Larry McReynolds.

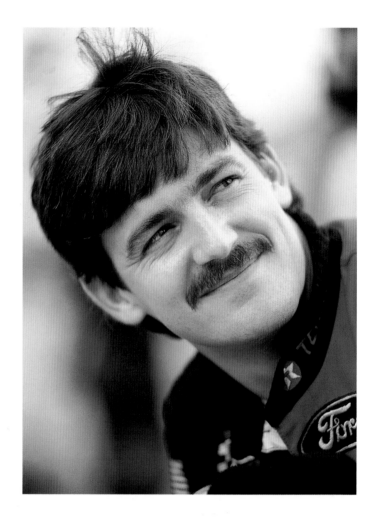

Watch how fast that serious
face turns to smiles and
laughter.

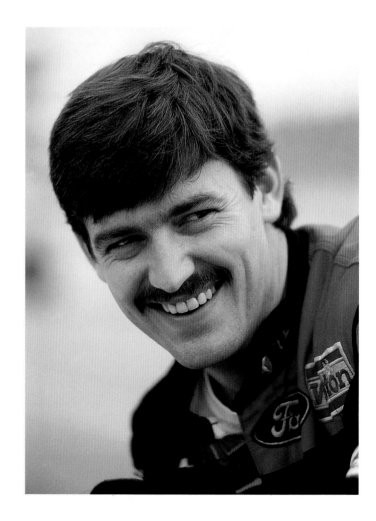

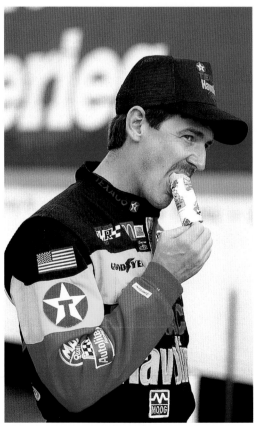

Davey's favorite pastime was eating ice cream. It was common to see Davey at the track with an ice cream in his hand or to see him chasing the ice cream cart down pit road.

I always said that Davey
was a man of many
faces. He had that magical
way of always making you
feel good with every look.
He would always keep you
guessing what was going
on in his head.

Liz Allison

(Above) In 1987, his rookie year in Winston Cup
racing, Davey watches as his fellow race car
drivers practice on the track. (Facing) This is the
smile that so many came to love.

Racing

Davey leads Bobby Hamilton out of turn three at Richmond International Raceway. Davey raced well at Richmond and considered it one of his favorite tracks.

The entire Davey Allison crew, including Robert Yates, car owner, and Larry McReynolds, crew chief, assembled for this February 23, 1991, team picture at Richmond International Raceway. Team member Howard Simerly (eighth person from left) died in December 1992.

59

(Facing) Davey does some fender banging at Martinsville in 1992. This is one of the few tracks where he never recorded a victory.

(Above) Davey enjoyed great communications with his crew chief, Larry McReynolds. The two of them never gave up. They spent hours at the track, trying one thing, then another, until they got it right. (Left) Davey and Larry kept a close eye on the other cars on the track. The two of them didn't miss much.

(Above) Robert Yates, Larry McReynolds, and Davey never missed a chance to discuss their race day game plan. The three of them worked well together, both on and off the track. (Right) Tommy Allison, Davey's cousin and business manager, shared Davey's Winston Cup dream. Together they achieved it. (Facing) Davey and Larry share a special victory hug. The win at Phoenix in 1992 put Davey back in the points lead going to Atlanta, the final race of the season.

*O*f all the wonderful, comical, and sometimes embarrassing incidents that I remember from my close relationship with Davey, one that sticks out in my mind happened during one of our first big wins together. It was May 1991. I had only been with the race team as a crew chief for about two months. One week earlier at Charlotte, we sat on the pole and led every lap to win the prestigious all-star race called The Winston.

Now it was late in the race during the World 600 at Charlotte. We had led all but just a few laps. We had a pretty good-sized lead at this point, but with it being the longest event of the season, you know that at any time something can happen to end your day. We had about 30 to 40 laps to go. We didn't even have to make another pit stop if there were no more caution flags.

I was getting a little nervous, since I really wasn't used to being in this situation. Davey wasn't saying much on the radio, which was normal under these circumstances. Davey really never got nervous about anything, but under these conditions he would just try and concentrate, run good, consistent laps, and not make any mistakes. About every five laps, I had been telling him his lap times, where the second-place car was, and how many laps were left to go.

All of a sudden on the radio Davey keyed his microphone and said, "Hey Larry, guess what's happening?"

At that point my heart went up through my throat because I just knew it was all over. We had either lost a cylinder in the engine, or a tire had

gone down, or something had gone amiss with something. So I frantically keyed my radio and asked, "What's wrong, Davey?"

You could tell by his voice that he knew he had rattled me and probably the rest of the crew. "You know," he said, "every time I come off turn two and go down the backstretch, there's this drunk Earnhardt fan hanging through the inside fence flipping me off, every lap."

I sighed with relief and replied, "Ten-four, Davey." Fortunately, we went on to win the race. As we were celebrating in Victory Lane, I grabbed him and hugged his neck, but I let him know I really could have done without the information about the Earnhardt fan. He just chuckled and grinned that famous Davey Allison grin, which let you know he was tickled to death he had gotten the best of you, which he did on a regular basis.

Larry McReynolds

(Above) Davey had a quick pit crew whose members took pride in their reputation as one of the best. (Facing) The Texaco/Havoline Ford Thunderbird piloted by Davey Allison.

(Above) Red Farmer and Davey go way back in Allison family history. Red and Bobby raced against each other and worked together, so Davey had known Red most of his life. When Davey purchased his Busch Grand National team, he hired Red as crew chief. Red Farmer was like a second father to Davey. (Right) Although Davey had a great pit crew, he still liked to get under the car and get his hands greasy. (Facing) Davey takes a turn at the 1991 Sears Point race in Sonoma, California, on his way to victory. I was pregnant with our second child, Robbie, at the time and watched this win from home.

(Above) A reflective moment with King Richard.
(Facing) Mark Martin, Alan Kulwicki, Davey,
and Bill Elliott pose for a picture on pit road.

(Facing) An historical moment —Davey and Alan Kulwicki battle for position at Atlanta Motor Speedway. (Above and left) Davey shares racing stories with Mark Martin and Wally Dallenbach, Jr.

*T*he friendship Davey and I shared will always be an important part of my life. I miss him very much.

Brett Bodine

There are few friends who meant as much to Davey and me as Brett and Diane Bodine. We shared many special moments together.

Jeff Gordon relaxes with Davey before a race.

(Above, top) Rusty Wallace, Davey, and Dale Jarrett share the podium during a press conference. (Above) Davey takes a parade lap with Sterling Marlin before a race. (Facing) Michael Waltrip, Davey, and Dale Jarrett go three wide.

(Facing) Davey, Geoff Bodine, Bobby Hamilton, and Bill Elliott wait impatiently for the Intimidator to get off the telephone.
(Below) Dale Earnhardt and Davey enjoyed racing against each other. Here Davey makes the pass.

(Above) Davey poses with other members of the International Race of Champions. Davey won the IROC championship posthumously in 1993.
(Right) Davey stops to talk with crew members after a Busch Grand National qualifying run. (Facing) At full speed.

(Above) Spending almost every weekend at the race-track makes everyone's children seem like your own. Here Davey gets a pre-race hug from Darrell and Stevie Waltrip's daughter, Jessica. (Right) Ned Jarrett interviews Davey. (Facing) Davey always tried to make time for his fans. At Pocono he signs autographs through the garage area fence.

(Above and right) Davey always said he had the best fans in the world. He enjoyed being asked to sign autographs and would try to stay until everyone had something signed.

(Above) Davey loved all his fans, big and small. He especially loved the children. He was involved in many children's charities, including Make-A-Wish Foundation and Dream Makers. It thrilled him to be able to bring joy to a child's life. (Left) Davey gives a wave and a big smile to some fans walking by.

Qualifying run at Watkins Glen. Davey developed his skills to the point where he felt comfortable driving the road courses, and usually finished well in these events. Although he never won at Watkins Glen, he did win at Sonoma, a twisting road course.

(Above) Davey wasn't a stranger to getting bumped around on the track, and was even known to take a tumble or two himself. (Facing) Because of the points battle for the championship, Davey would come back on the racetrack in all sorts of conditions to get the best finish possible. There were times when he had some ugly cars on the track!

Unfortunately, Davey suffered a number of injuries. Here he crawls out of his car at Bristol International Raceway after a painful accident. He climbs out with little hesitation, even though his ribs are broken.

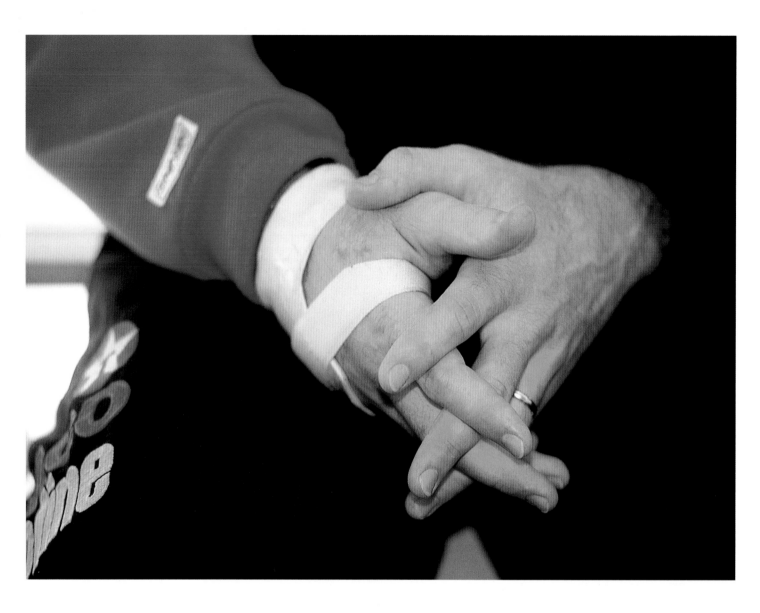

In spite of the injuries, Davey
never gave up.

Phoenix
International
Raceway
TEXACO
Havoline
FORMULA 3
SAE
Motor Oil

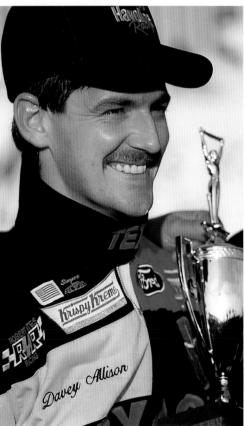

Davey loved nothing more about racing than winning. He did both so well. These are a few of his victories.

(Above and facing) After winning the Miller Genuine Draft race in Michigan, Davey's crew members were very excited about pouring a huge Miller beer over his head in Victory Lane. Joey Knuckles, Davey's longtime friend and crew member, gets a big laugh out of the action.

(Above) Davey in Victory Lane at Talladega in 1992 after winning the IROC event. Victories at Talladega were always the best because all our family would be there. (Right) This picture is very special to me. Bristol in 1990 was my first trip to Victory Lane. Davey had won other races while we were dating and after we were married, but somehow I always ended up not being there. I'll always cherish that Bristol win. (Facing) Davey poses with his IROC trophy after winning at Darlington in 1993.

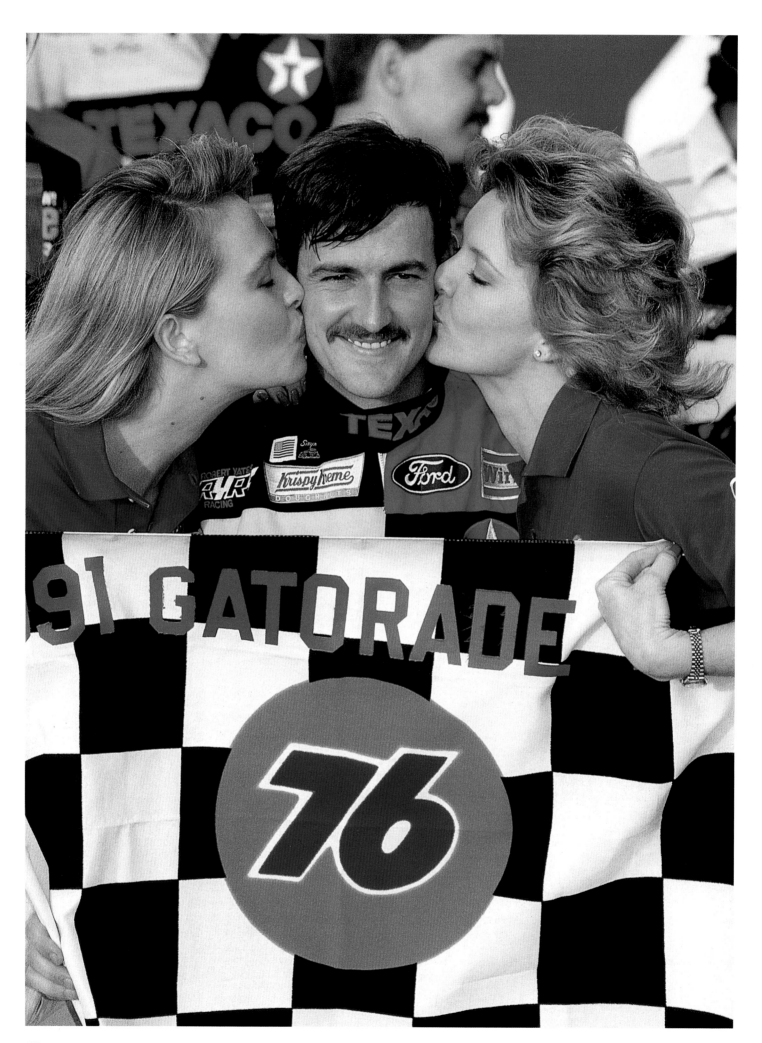

One of Davey's favorite parts of going to Victory Lane was getting kissed by the beautiful UNOCAL RaceStoppers.

Off the track

Davey was good at most everything, including softball. Here he plays in a celebrity game to raise money for a fellow racer who had been injured in an accident.

(Right) Davey was an avid hunter. He is proudly displaying a buck he shot and had mounted. It hangs on the wall in my study at home. (Facing) Davey loved fishing and jumped on every opportunity to participate in a fishing tournament. Here he shows off a twenty-six pound striped bass he caught at Smith Lake, which is outside Birmingham. He had been fishing with Mike Bolton, a friend and journalist from a Birmingham newspaper.

Family and friends

Davey, Clifford, and Bobby pose for a picture at Bristol International Raceway in 1992. Bobby, Clifford's wife, Elisa, and I have this picture hanging in our homes. As far as we know, it is the last one taken of the three of them together.

(Above) Davey with his cousin, Tommy Allison. (Facing) Davey talks with Tommy, Greg Campbell, Charlie Brock, and Sam Manze. I'd be afraid to know what they're saying. Together they could come up with some crazy stuff.

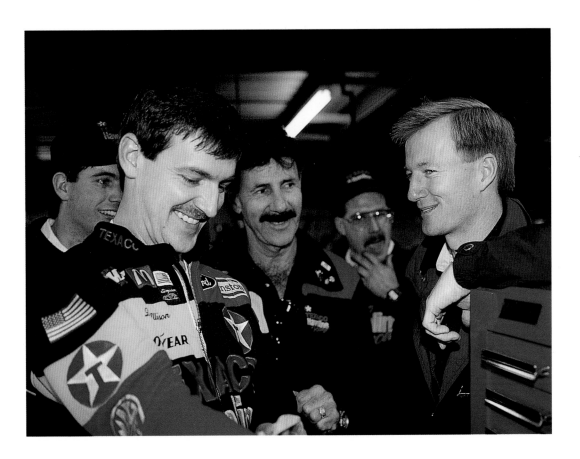

I have many fond memories of Davey from the time we were old enough to speak, to the time of his passing. One memory that stands out comes from November 1992. That was a year of many highs and lows. The race in Phoenix brought another high. It was his first victory since his accident at Pocono. After the race we made the trip back to Hueytown, and arrived early Monday morning. I drove Davey to the shop to pick up his truck. During the ride home from the airport we talked about the ups and downs of the year and how nice it was to be back in Winner's Circle. When I dropped him off he looked over at me and thanked me for being a part of his life. That will stick with me forever.

Tommy Allison

(Facing) Clifford with his "grizzly beard," as Davey called it. The two of them had always loved each other as brothers, but during the last years of their lives they became even closer. Davey wanted Clifford to have the chance he deserved as a race car driver. Davey often said that Clifford was born with more racing talent than he was. He knew in time that Clifford would be a great NASCAR driver. (Above) Davey and Clifford loved talking about racing. They didn't always agree, but they had fun discussing it. (Left) Tommy places an "In Memory of Clifford Allison" sticker on Davey's car after Clifford's death. All the drivers at Michigan carried the same decal.

(Above) Our son Robbie was baptized in a dual ceremony. Davey and I were asked to be the godparents of Larry and Linda McReynolds's son, Brandon, and we asked them to be Robbie's godparents. The only time we could get everyone together was during Race Week at Charlotte in October 1991. Father Dale Grubba baptized our children in the tower at Charlotte Motor Speedway. (Facing, above) Davey and I renewed our wedding vows in January 1993 at St. Aloysius Catholic Church in Bessemer, Alabama. Pictured here are (left to right) my father, Grey Mayson; myself, holding Robbie; Davey, holding Krista; my mother, Betty Mayson; and my grandmother, Edna Walters. (Facing, below) Davey's two beautiful sisters, Bonnie (right) and Carrie (left), were so special to him. Here they celebrate Bonnie's wedding to Bubba Farr in 1992.

(Above) Davey, Krista, and I pose with President George Bush at Daytona International Speedway. (Right) Davey was a huge fan of the San Francisco 49ers and especially of Joe Montana, who at the time was still playing for the team. On Davey's truck they discuss the ins and outs of racing. (Facing) Davey shares a laugh with his uncle, Donnie Allison. The two were very close and enjoyed their time together on and off the track. Davey spent a lot of time at Uncle Donnie's farm.

Husband and father

One of my most cherished pictures. Simpson Race Products made driver's suits to fit Robbie and Krista. Robbie is only five months old and Krista is eating a handful of Cheerios. If you look closely you can see one in her hand.

(Above) Davey was an affectionate person and loved getting big hugs before a race. Here we are at North Wilkesboro Speedway in 1991. I was pregnant with Robbie at the time. (Facing) Callaway Gardens near Columbus, Georgia, was our favorite getaway spot. We often spent holidays and off weekends there. Callaway holds precious memories for Robbie, Krista, and me.

(Facing) I always made it a point to walk Davey out to his car for the start of a race. Here we cruise down pit road for the night race at Richmond, one of Davey's favorite events. (Above) Before every race Max Helton leads a prayer service for drivers, crew members, and their families. Davey and I are attending the service before the Richmond race.

(Above, top) Some days are just not as good as others. You can see how disappointed we are about the events of a day at Michigan. (Above) On mornings before a race Davey would take some quiet time and maybe even a nap. I would bring him lunch about an hour before the start of the race. As you can see, he enjoyed being pampered. (Facing) We share a few words before the start of a race at Talladega. Those few minutes with Davey before a race were precious. Sometimes he was serious, but most of the time he was a clown. He was like a kid getting ready to do something he loved.

(Above) Davey and I pose with the Texaco/Havoline Ford Thunderbird Racing Team at Atlanta Motor Speedway. (Right) I loved Davey winning as much as he loved winning. Victory Lane was always a great place to be. Here we hold the checkered flag at Talladega in 1992. (Facing) My favorite part of Victory Lane. Krista seemed to like it, too.

125

Davey and Robbie share a moment as father and son. There is nothing like the love a man has for his children. When Krista and Robbie were born, a whole new side of Davey emerged. It was very important to him for the children and me to be at the races. I often saw scenes just like this one.

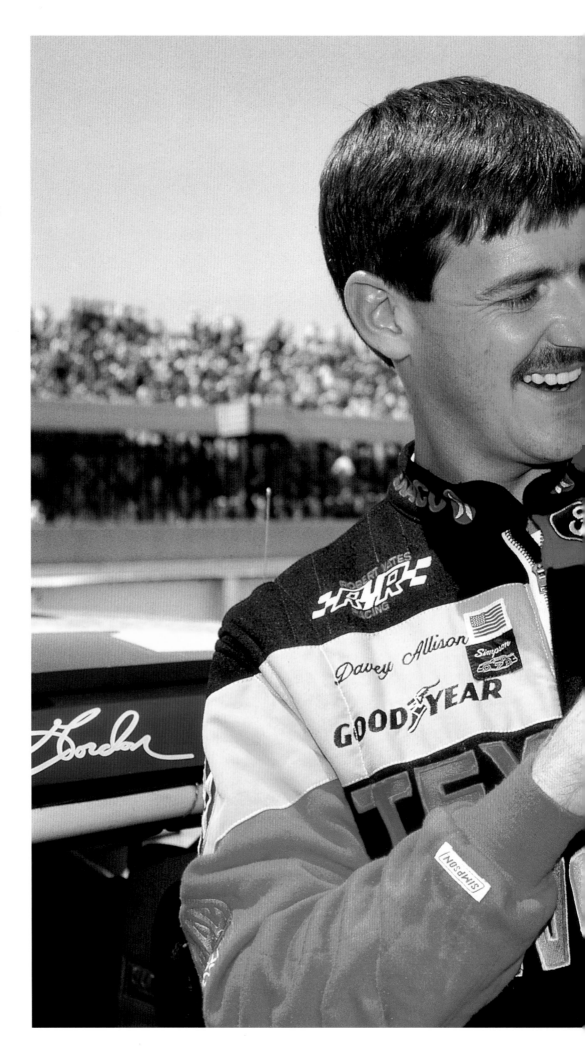

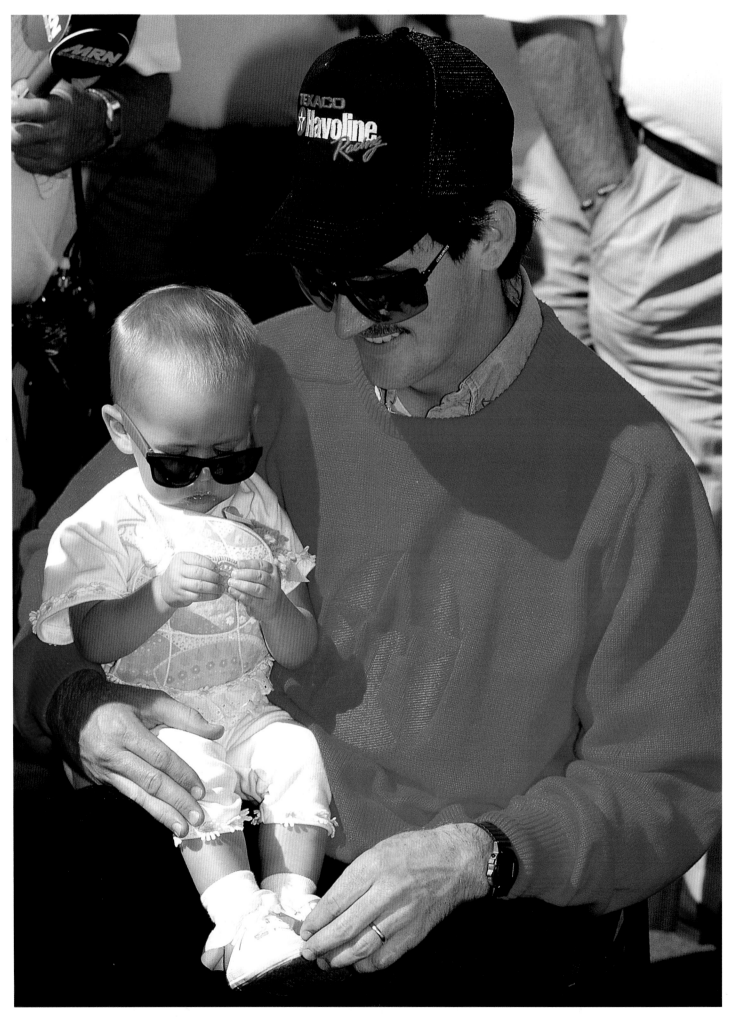

(Facing) Davey holds Krista as they check out her new shades. Davey had just bought sunglasses for Krista and she loved them. (Above) A typical race Sunday—any mom can relate. I had to start at the hotel at 6:00 A.M. to get to pit road by the start of the race. It was quite a feat, but it was worth every crazy minute. (Left) Davey gets a big Victory Lane kiss from Krista at Rockingham.

(Facing, above) Victory Lane after Davey won the Daytona 500. The children are a little overwhelmed, but it didn't take them long to catch on that Victory Lane is where you want to be. (Facing, below) Robbie gives Daddy a good-luck hug before the Pocono race in June 1993. (Left) Krista rides on Daddy's shoulders and pulls his hair, which gets a big smile from Davey. (Below) Krista decides at Martinsville Speedway that she should drive the race car. She wouldn't get out and, of course, Dad thought that was great.

(Facing) Robbie and Davey clown around before driver introduction. There's no mistaking that Allison smile. (Above) At our home in Hueytown, Alabama, the children loved to climb up in that chair and cuddle with Daddy. Sometimes it was for games, sometimes to watch a movie together, but always to be close to the Daddy they loved.

(Above) Davey's Christmas present in 1992. We were building our home, with a playroom planned for the children. We decided to use a racing motif. I found someone to make a carpet with Davey's racing logo and surprised him with the finished product. (Facing) These gates lead into the home Davey and I built for our family. Davey designed the house and the lakes behind it. He was very proud of his work. After a year of construction, we moved into our home in January 1993.

Final tribute

Davey ran his last race at New Hampshire International Speedway. The children and I did not attend. Many of you will remember that in his post-race interview, Davey said hello to Krista and Robbie, and said he would be home soon.

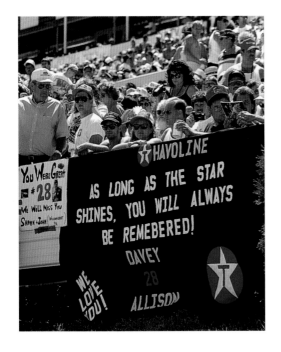

(Facing, above) This billboard was put up in Birmingham the day of Davey's death. Billboards and signs appeared all over the Birmingham area. Hundreds of cars rode with their headlights on, paying tribute to their hometown hero. (Facing, below) The Robert Yates Racing Team withdrew from the Pocono race, which took place only days after Davey's death. To pay their respects, truck drivers from all the teams placed this wreath where the #28 truck would have been parked. (Above) The fans will never know how much their support helped the family through this difficult time. Every sign, banner, poster, and the many expressions of love that were shown for Davey will never be forgotten.

(Above) When Dale Earnhardt won the race at Pocono the weekend following Davey's death, his team met at the finish line for a prayer and a moment of silence. Then Dale took his victory lap carrying Davey's flag. (Right) Throughout the '93 season the family of racing honored Davey on their cars and uniforms, and in their minds and hearts. We are grateful to you all.

DAVEY ALLISON

Full Name David Carl Allison. **Birthdate** February 25, 1961. **Birthplace** Hollywood, Florida. **Height** 5'9". **Weight** 160 lbs. **Residence** Hueytown, Alabama. **Wife** "Liz" (formerly Elizabeth Mayson). **Children** Krista Marie, December 24, 1989. Robert (Robbie) Grey, July 30, 1991.

1973 Began at age 12 sweeping floors, sorting nuts and bolts at father's shop, Bobby Allison Racing (BAR), for 50 cents a hour. **1979** Completed high school and started full time at BAR. Used shop and equipment to build first race car, but only after 5:00 P.M. Constructed 1967 Chevrolet Nova from ground up. Started first race on April 22 in Birmingham. Drove borrowed 1972 Chevrolet II Nova. Finished fifth in 20-lap Limited Sportsman feature. Won first race in sixth start, at Birmingham on May 5, with Dad in pits. **1983** Earned first superspeedway pole and victory in ARCA race at Talladega on April 30. Started first Busch Grand National race at Rockingham, NC, on March 5 and finished 25th. **1984** Named ARCA Rookie of the Year. Started first Winston Cup race at Talladega 500 on July 28. Qualified 22nd and finished 10th in Hoss Ellington's Lancaster Tobacco Chevrolet, won $6,025. **1987** Hired by Ranier/Lundy Winston Cup team. Qualified second at 209+ MPH to become first rookie to start on front row for Daytona 500. Began driving under Texaco sponsorship. Won first Winston Cup race at Talladega on May 3. Became only driver in Winston Cup history to win twice in rookie season. Earned Rookie of the Year. Founded Davey Allison Racing Enterprises Busch Grand National team in December. **1988** Finished second to father, Bobby, at Daytona 500. Won third Winston Cup race at Michigan on August 21 and from pole at Richmond on September 11. Finished eighth in Winston Cup points, won $844,532. Team became Robert Yates Racing on October 1, when Yates purchased operation from Harry Ranier. **1989** Earned fifth Winston Cup victory by winning Talladega on May 7 for second time. Posted sixth win at Daytona on July 1. Finished 11th in Winston Cup points, won $640,956. **1990** Scored two more Winston Cup wins, at Bristol on April 8 and at Charlotte on October 7. Finished 13th in Winston Cup points, won $640,684. **1991** Claimed five victories and won The Winston all-star race from pole. Davey led more races (23), more times (73), for more miles (1,879.12) than any other Winston Cup driver. Finished third in final standings and won career high $1,732,924. **1992** Despite wrecking primary car in practice, rebounded to win season-opening Daytona 500. Joined father,

DAVEY ALLISON CAREER HIGHLIGHTS

1983	Bill France Triple Crown Award-ARCA
1984	ARCA Rookie of the Year
1987	Winston Cup Rookie of the Year
1988	Alabama Sportsman of the Year
1991/1992	The Winston All-Star Race Winner
1991/1992	True Value Hard Charger
1992	Daytona 500 Winner
1992	NMPA Richard Petty Driver of the Year
1993	Super Ford Magazine Driver of the Year
1993	IROC Champion
1995	Inducted into Alabama Sports Hall of Fame

Won 14 pole positions and 19 races in 191 career starts. Won at least two races in every Winston Cup Season in which he competed. Only driver to win two races and five poles in rookie season.

DAVEY ALLISON WINSTON CUP WINS

Win #	Date	Track	Car Owner
1	05/03/87	Talladega, AL	Ranier/Lundy
2	05/31/87	Dover, DE	Ranier/Lundy
3	08/21/88	Brooklyn, MI	Harry Ranier
4	09/11/88	Richmond, VA	Harry Ranier
5	05/07/89	Talladega, AL	Robert Yates Racing
6	07/01/89	Daytona Beach, FL	Robert Yates Racing
7	04/08/90	Bristol, TN	Robert Yates Racing
8	10/08/90	Charlotte, NC	Robert Yates Racing
8A	02/14/91	Daytona Beach, FL	Robert Yates Racing
8B	05/19/91	Charlotte, NC	Robert Yates Racing
9	05/26/91	Charlotte, NC	Robert Yates Racing
10	06/09/91	Sears Point, CA	Robert Yates Racing
11	06/23/91	Brooklyn, MI	Robert Yates Racing
12	10/20/91	Rockingham, NC	Robert Yates Racing
13	11/03/91	Phoenix, AZ	Robert Yates Racing
14	02/16/92	Daytona Beach, FL	Robert Yates Racing
15	04/12/92	No. Wilkesboro, NC	Robert Yates Racing
16	05/03/92	Talladega, AL	Robert Yates Racing
16A	05/16/92	Charlotte, NC	Robert Yates Racing
17	06/21/92	Brooklyn, MI	Robert Yates Racing
18	11/01/92	Phoenix, AZ	Robert Yates Racing
19	03/07/93	Richmond, VA	Robert Yates Racing

#8A was a qualifying race. #8B was an All-Star event. #16A was an All-Star event. These three races were non-points events and did not count as Winston Cup wins.

Bobby, a three-time winner, to become second father-son duo (Lee-Richard Petty) to win the 500. Led 50 laps at Bristol, before an oil-line fitting broke and sent his car skating into the wall on April 5. Separated cartilage, fractured ribs, bruised lung, and tore ligaments and muscles in his right shoulder. Due to Davey's injuries, Jimmy Hensley qualified car at North Wilkesboro, NC. Davey grabbed lead with 87 laps to go and, despite severe leg cramps, held off Rusty Wallace for the victory on April 12. Led 110 of 188 laps to win Winston 500 at Talladega on May 3. Started from pole, led 160 of 200 laps and won Brooklyn, MI, on June 21. Despite spending two nights in a Charlotte hospital for treatment of a virus, sped to pole and led 115 laps at Pocono on July 19 before contact with Darrell Waltrip on lap 149 sent car into a spectacular, 11-flip accident. That night, surgeons installed two plates in his broken forearm and pins in his dislocated, shattered wrist. Also sustained a broken collarbone and severe swelling and bruising of his face and head. Six days later, practiced at 188+ MPH in preparation for race at Talladega on July 26. Relief driver Bobby Hillin qualified car third. Davey started, then yielded to Hillin for a third-place finish. Resurged to win at Phoenix on November 1 to regain Winston Cup points lead by 30 over Alan Kulwicki. Running sixth in the final race of the season with fewer than 100 laps to go and in position to secure the title, Davey was caught in an accident triggered by another driver. The wreck deprived him of the Winston Cup title and dropped him to third in points, his lowest ranking of the season. Led series in victories (tied at five), top-five finishes (17), laps led (1,362), miles led (2,315), and times led (tied at 50). **1993** After starting from 14th position, Davey won at Richmond on March 7. Finished third at Loudon, New Hampshire, in what would be his last race. Lost his life in a helicopter accident at Talladega Superspeedway on July 13. Posthumously named IROC Champion. **1995** On February 25, named to the Alabama Sports Hall of Fame.

DAVEY ALLISON BUSCH GRAND NATIONAL CAREER

Race	Date	Track	Owner	Sponsor	Start	Finish	Car
1.	03/05/83	Rockingham, NC	Nathan Sims			25	
2.	04/09/83	Darlington, SC	Nathan Sims				
3.	05/28/83	Charlotte, NC	Nathan Sims			14	9	
4.	09/04/83	Darlington, SC	Nathan Sims				4	
5.	10/08/83	Charlotte, NC	Nathan Sims			9	7	
6.	02/18/84	Daytona Beach, FL	Frank Plessinger		16	28	
7.	03/03/84	Rockingham, NC	Frank Plessinger		7	6	
8.	05/13/84	Milwaukee, WI	Bill Collins		4	5	
9.	05/19/84	Dover, DE	Bill Collins		5	4	
10.	10/06/84	Charlotte, NC	Bill Collins		22	35	
11.	10/20/84	Rockingham, NC	Bill Collins		14	28	
12.	02/16/85	Daytona Beach, FL	Bill Collins		26	38	
13.	04/13/85	Darlington, SC	Bill Collins		18	7	
14.	05/18/85	Dover, DE	Bill Collins		15	22	
15.	10/05/85	Charlotte, NC	Bill Collins		7	40	
16.	02/15/86	Daytona Beach, FL	BAR, Inc.		4	34	
17.	03/01/86	Rockingham, NC	BAR, Inc.		6	20	
18.	04/12/86	Darlington, SC	BAR, Inc.		10	5	
19.	05/12/86	Dover, DE	BAR, Inc.		3	29	
20.	05/24/86	Charlotte, NC	BAR, Inc.		2	3	
21.	07/06/86	Road Atlanta, GA	Ed Whitaker		7	25	
22.	07/19/86	South Boston, VA	Ed Whitaker		24	23	
23.	08/22/86	Bristol, TN	Ed Whitaker		10	5	
24.	08/30/86	Darlington, SC	BAR, Inc.		3	25	
25.	09/06/86	Richmond, VA	Ed Whitaker		24	25	
26.	09/20/86	Martinsville, VA	Ed Whitaker			30	
27.	10/04/86	Charlotte, NC	BAR, Inc.		8	9	
28.	10/18/86	Rockingham, NC	BAR, Inc.		1	2	
29.	02/13/88	Daytona Beach, FL	DARE, Inc.	Texaco/Havoline	38	6	Ford
30.	03/04/88	Rockingham, NC	DARE, Inc.	Texaco/Havoline	16	29	Buick
31.	03/05/88	Rockingham, NC	DARE, Inc.	Texaco/Havoline	29	13	Ford
32.	03/26/88	Darlington, SC	DARE, Inc.	Texaco/Havoline	26	40	Ford
33.	05/07/88	Nazareth, PA	DARE, Inc.	Texaco/Havoline	29	30	Ford
34.	08/06/88	Indianapolis, IN	DARE, Inc.	Texaco/Havoline	13	28	Buick
35.	08/26/88	Bristol, TN	DARE, Inc.	Texaco/Havoline	8	7	Buick
36.	09/03/88	Darlington, SC	DARE, Inc.	Texaco/Havoline	14	4	Buick
37.	09/17/88	Dover, DE	DARE, Inc.	Texaco/Havoline	8	10	Buick
38.	10/22/88	Rockingham, NC	DARE, Inc.	Texaco/Havoline	4	3	Buick
39.	04/01/89	Darlington, SC	DARE, Inc.	Texaco/Havoline	27	7	Buick
40.	04/30/89	Nazareth, PA	DARE, Inc.	Texaco/Havoline	7	5	Buick
41.	05/27/89	Charlotte, NC	DARE, Inc.	Texaco/Havoline	39	31	Buick
42.	08/05/89	Indianapolis, IN	DARE, Inc.	Texaco/Havoline	6	29	Buick
43.	08/25/89	Bristol, TN	DARE, Inc.	Texaco/Havoline	3	14	Buick
44.	09/02/89	Darlington, SC	DARE, Inc.	Texaco/Havoline	6	29	Ford
45.	09/09/89	Richmond, VA	DARE, Inc.	Texaco/Havoline	5	32	Ford
46.	10/21/89	Rockingham, NC	DARE, Inc.	Texaco/Havoline	16	26	Buick
47.	03/31/90	Darlington, SC	DARE, Inc.	DARE, Inc.			Chevrolet
48.	05/12/90	Nazareth, PA	DARE, Inc.	DARE, Inc.	1	10	Chevrolet
49.	05/26/90	Charlotte, NC	DARE, Inc.	DARE, Inc.	5	6	Chevrolet
50.	05/28/90	Charlotte, NC	DARE, Inc.	Texaco/Havoline	39	40	Ford
51.	08/04/90	Indianapolis, IN	DARE, Inc.	DARE, Inc.			Chevrolet
52.	08/24/90	Bristol, TN	DARE, Inc.	DARE, Inc.	21	8	Chevrolet
53.	09/01/90	Darlington, SC	DARE, Inc.	DARE, Inc.	6	7	Chevrolet
54.	09/08/90	Richmond, VA	DARE, Inc.	Autolite	17	26	Chevrolet
55.	10/06/90	Charlotte, NC	DARE, Inc.	Texaco/Havoline	31	31	Chevrolet
56.	10/14/90	Loudon, NH	DARE, Inc.	Texaco/Havoline	7	16	Chevrolet
57.	10/20/90	Rockingham, NC	DARE, Inc.	Texaco/Havoline	11	6	Chevrolet
58.	02/16/91	Daytona Beach, FL	DARE, Inc.	Texaco/Havoline	7	3	Chevrolet
59.	02/23/91	Richmond, VA	DARE, Inc.	Texaco/Havoline	7	10	Chevrolet
60.	03/02/91	Rockingham, NC	DARE, Inc.	Texaco/Havoline	23	34	Chevrolet
61.	04/13/91	Bristol, TN	DARE, Inc.	Texaco/Havoline	15	11	Chevrolet
62.	05/11/91	Nazareth, PA	DARE, Inc.	Texaco/Havoline	14	30	Chevrolet
63.	05/25/91	Charlotte, NC	DARE, Inc.	Texaco/Havoline	16	36	Chevrolet
64.	06/01/91	Dover, DE	DARE, Inc.	Texaco/Havoline	30	6	Chevrolet
65.	07/14/91	Loudon, NH	DARE, Inc.	Texaco/Havoline	5	30	Buick
66.	08/23/91	Bristol, TN	DARE, Inc.	Texaco/Havoline	25	4	Buick
67.	08/31/91	Darlington, SC	DARE, Inc.	Texaco/Havoline	9	34	Buick
68.	09/06/91	Richmond, VA	DARE, Inc.	Texaco/Havoline	31	21	Buick
69.	10/05/91	Charlotte, NC	DARE, Inc.	Texaco/Havoline	39	37	Buick
70.	10/13/91	Loudon, NH	DARE, Inc.	Texaco/Havoline	9	44	Buick
71.	10/19/91	Rockingham, NC	DARE, Inc.	Texaco/Havoline	3	35	Buick
72.	02/15/92	Daytona Beach, FL	DARE, Inc.	Texaco/Havoline	20	12	Ford
73.	02/29/92	Rockingham, NC	DARE, Inc.	Texaco/Havoline	14	3	Ford
74.	03/07/92	Richmond, VA	DARE, Inc.	Texaco/Havoline	18	25	Ford
75.	03/14/92	Atlanta, GA	DARE, Inc.	Texaco/Havoline	19	4	Ford
76.	03/28/92	Darlington, SC	DARE, Inc.	Texaco/Havoline	18	34	Ford
77.	04/04/92	Bristol, TN	DARE, Inc.	Texaco/Havoline	19	2	Ford
78.	07/12/92	Loudon, NH	DARE, Inc.	Texaco/Havoline	3	32	Ford
79.	02/13/93	Daytona Beach, FL	DARE, Inc.	Mac Tools/Havoline	27	36	Ford
80.	02/27/93	Rockingham, NC	DARE, Inc.	Mac Tools/Havoline	26	35	Ford
81.	03/06/93	Richmond, VA	DARE, Inc.	Mac Tools/Havoline	15	31	Ford
82.	03/27/93	Darlington, SC	DARE, Inc.	Mac Tools/Havoline	36	13	Ford
83.	05/29/93	Charlotte, NC	DARE, Inc.	Mac Tools/Havoline	28	30	Ford
84.	07/04/93	Milwaukee, WI	DARE, Inc.	Mac Tools/Havoline	23	27	Ford

DAVEY ALLISON WINSTON CUP CAREER

Race	Date	Track	Owner	Sponsor	Start	Finish	Car
1.	07/28/85	Talladega, AL	Hoss Ellington	Lancaster Tobacco	22	10	Chevrolet
2.	10/06/85	Charlotte, NC	Hoss Ellington	Lancaster Tobacco	17	19	Chevrolet
3.	11/03/85	Atlanta, GA	Hoss Ellington	Lancaster Tobacco	32	42	Chevrolet
4.	02/23/86	Richmond, VA	Sadler Brothers		28	12	Chevrolet
5.	04/13/86	Bristol, TN	Sadler Brothers		26	39	Chevrolet
6.	06/04/86	Darlington, SC	Sadler Brothers		29	20	Chevrolet
7.	07/27/86	Talladega, AL	Junior Johnson	Budweiser	7	7	Chevrolet
8.	09/02/86	Rockingham, NC	Sadler Brothers		26	25	Chevrolet
9.	02/15/87	Daytona Beach, FL	Harry Ranier	Texaco/Havoline	2	27	Ford
10.	03/01/87	Rockingham, NC	Harry Ranier	Texaco/Havoline	1	9	Ford
11.	03/08/87	Richmond, VA	Harry Ranier	Texaco/Havoline	21	26	Ford
12.	03/15/87	Atlanta, GA	Harry Ranier	Texaco/Havoline	8	5	Ford
13.	03/29/87	Darlington, SC	Harry Ranier	Texaco/Havoline	5	27	Ford
14.	05/03/87	Talladega, AL	Harry Ranier	Texaco/Havoline	3	1	Ford
15.	05/24/87	Charlotte, NC	Harry Ranier	Texaco/Havoline	16	16	Ford
16.	05/31/87	Dover, DE	Harry Ranier	Texaco/Havoline	2	1	Ford
17.	06/14/87	Pocono, PA	Harry Ranier	Texaco/Havoline	26	12	Ford
18.	06/28/87	Brooklyn, MI	Harry Ranier	Texaco/Havoline	7	2	Ford
19.	07/04/87	Daytona Beach, FL	Harry Ranier	Texaco/Havoline	1	20	Ford
20.	07/19/87	Pocono, PA	Harry Ranier	Texaco/Havoline	6	5	Ford
21.	07/26/87	Talladega, AL	Harry Ranier	Texaco/Havoline	3	2	Ford
22.	08/09/87	Watkins Glen, NY	Harry Ranier	Texaco/Havoline	33	17	Ford
23.	08/16/87	Brooklyn, MI	Harry Ranier	Texaco/Havoline	1	5	Ford
24.	09/06/87	Darlington, SC	Harry Ranier	Texaco/Havoline	1	29	Ford
25.	09/20/87	Dover, DE	Harry Ranier	Texaco/Havoline	2	2	Ford
26.	10/04/87	No. Wilkesboro, NC	Harry Ranier	Texaco/Havoline	22	26	Ford
27.	10/11/87	Charlotte, NC	Harry Ranier	Texaco/Havoline	10	19	Ford
28.	10/25/87	Rockingham, NC	Harry Ranier	Texaco/Havoline	1	42	Ford
29.	11/08/87	Riverside, CA	Harry Ranier	Texaco/Havoline	25	14	Ford
30.	11/22/87	Atlanta, GA	Harry Ranier	Texaco/Havoline	5	5	Ford
31.	02/14/88	Daytona Beach, FL	Harry Ranier	Texaco/Havoline	2	2	Ford
32.	02/21/88	Richmond, VA	Harry Ranier	Texaco/Havoline	15	29	Ford
33.	03/06/88	Rockingham, NC	Harry Ranier	Texaco/Havoline	4	9	Ford
34.	03/20/88	Atlanta, GA	Harry Ranier	Texaco/Havoline	41	40	Ford
35.	03/27/88	Darlington, SC	Harry Ranier	Texaco/Havoline	9	3	Ford
36.	04/10/88	Bristol, TN	Harry Ranier	Texaco/Havoline	19	29	Ford
37.	04/17/88	No. Wilkesboro, NC	Harry Ranier	Texaco/Havoline	20	8	Ford
38.	04/24/88	Martinsville, VA	Harry Ranier	Texaco/Havoline	26	6	Ford
39.	05/01/88	Talladega, AL	Harry Ranier	Texaco/Havoline	1	34	Ford
40.	05/29/88	Charlotte, NC	Harry Ranier	Texaco/Havoline	5	5	Ford
41.	06/05/88	Dover, DE	Harry Ranier	Texaco/Havoline	14	5	Ford
42.	06/12/88	Riverside, CA	Harry Ranier	Texaco/Havoline	34	32	Ford
43.	06/19/88	Pocono, PA	Harry Ranier	Texaco/Havoline	6	5	Ford
44.	06/26/88	Brooklyn, MI	Harry Ranier	Texaco/Havoline	3	35	Ford
45.	07/02/88	Daytona Beach, FL	Harry Ranier	Texaco/Havoline	3	38	Ford
46.	07/24/88	Pocono, PA	Harry Ranier	Texaco/Havoline	12	3	Ford
47.	07/31/88	Talladega, AL	Harry Ranier	Texaco/Havoline	3	39	Ford
48.	08/14/88	Watkins Glen, NY	Harry Ranier	Texaco/Havoline	28	16	Ford
49.	08/21/88	Brooklyn, MI	Harry Ranier	Texaco/Havoline	4	1	Ford
50.	08/27/88	Bristol, TN	Harry Ranier	Texaco/Havoline	11	4	Ford
51.	09/04/88	Darlington, SC	Harry Ranier	Texaco/Havoline	15	9	Ford

Race	Date	Track	Owner	Sponsor	Start	Finish	Car
52.	09/11/88	Richmond, VA	Harry Ranier	Texaco/Havoline	1	1	Ford
53.	09/18/88	Dover, DE	Harry Ranier	Texaco/Havoline	10	4	Ford
54.	09/25/88	Martinsville, VA	Harry Ranier	Texaco/Havoline	22	18	Ford
55.	10/09/88	Charlotte, NC	Harry Ranier	Texaco/Havoline	14	19	Ford
56.	10/16/88	No. Wilkesboro, NC	Harry Ranier	Texaco/Havoline	13	11	Ford
57.	10/23/88	Rockingham, NC	Harry Ranier	Texaco/Havoline	6	27	Ford
58.	11/06/88	Phoenix, AZ	Harry Ranier	Texaco/Havoline	20	3	Ford
59.	11/20/88	Atlanta, GA	Harry Ranier	Texaco/Havoline	23	2	Ford
60.	02/19/89	Daytona Beach, FL	RYR	Texaco/Havoline	16	25	Ford
61.	03/05/89	Rockingham, NC	RYR	Texaco/Havoline	17	6	Ford
62.	03/19/89	Atlanta, GA	RYR	Texaco/Havoline	9	40	Ford
63.	03/26/89	Richmond, VA	RYR	Texaco/Havoline	35	5	Ford
64.	04/02/89	Darlington, SC	RYR	Texaco/Havoline	4	2	Ford
65.	04/09/89	Bristol, TN	RYR	Texaco/Havoline	31	4	Ford
66.	04/16/89	No. Wilkesboro, NC	RYR	Texaco/Havoline	17	11	Ford
67.	04/23/89	Martinsville, VA	RYR	Texaco/Havoline	28	14	Ford
68.	05/07/89	Talladega, AL	RYR	Texaco/Havoline	2	1	Ford
69.	05/28/89	Charlotte, NC	RYR	Texaco/Havoline	17	33	Ford
70.	06/04/89	Dover, DE	RYR	Texaco/Havoline	22	32	Ford
71.	06/11/89	Sears Point, CA	RYR	Texaco/Havoline	15	9	Ford
72.	06/18/89	Pocono, PA	RYR	Texaco/Havoline	27	16	Ford
73.	06/25/89	Brooklyn, MI	RYR	Texaco/Havoline	10	31	Ford
74.	07/01/89	Daytona Beach, FL	RYR	Texaco/Havoline	8	1	Ford
75.	07/23/89	Pocono, PA	RYR	Texaco/Havoline	23	6	Ford
76.	07/30/89	Talladega, AL	RYR	Texaco/Havoline	7	9	Ford
77.	08/13/89	Watkins Glen, NY	RYR	Texaco/Havoline	21	4	Ford
78.	08/20/89	Brooklyn, MI	RYR	Texaco/Havoline	11	7	Ford
79.	08/26/89	Bristol, TN	RYR	Texaco/Havoline	20	25	Ford
80.	09/03/89	Darlington, SC	RYR	Texaco/Havoline	25	18	Ford
81.	09/10/89	Richmond, VA	RYR	Texaco/Havoline	5	10	Ford
82.	09/17/89	Dover, DE	RYR	Texaco/Havoline	1	24	Ford
83.	09/24/89	Martinsville, VA	RYR	Texaco/Havoline	17	21	Ford
84.	10/08/89	Charlotte, NC	RYR	Texaco/Havoline	5	5	Ford
85.	10/15/89	No. Wilkesboro, NC	RYR	Texaco/Havoline	8	21	Ford
86.	10/22/89	Rockingham, NC	RYR	Texaco/Havoline	13	26	Ford
87.	11/05/89	Phoenix, AZ	RYR	Texaco/Havoline	14	39	Ford
88.	11/19/89	Atlanta, GA	RYR	Texaco/Havoline	18	25	Ford
89.	02/18/90	Daytona Beach, FL	RYR	Texaco/Havoline	16	20	Ford
90.	02/25/90	Richmond, VA	RYR	Texaco/Havoline	31	20	Ford
91.	03/04/90	Rockingham, NC	RYR	Texaco/Havoline	18	34	Ford
92.	03/18/90	Atlanta, GA	RYR	Texaco/Havoline	28	13	Ford
93.	04/01/90	Darlington, SC	RYR	Texaco/Havoline	13	3	Ford
94.	04/08/90	Bristol, TN	RYR	Texaco/Havoline	19	1	Ford
95.	04/22/90	No. Wilkesboro, NC	RYR	Texaco/Havoline	17	9	Ford
96.	04/29/90	Martinsville, VA	RYR	Texaco/Havoline	19	22	Ford
97.	05/06/90	Talladega, AL	RYR	Texaco/Havoline	8	25	Ford
98.	05/27/90	Charlotte, NC	RYR	Texaco/Havoline	6	7	Ford
99.	06/03/90	Dover, DE	RYR	Texaco/Havoline	27	17	Ford
100.	06/10/90	Sears Point, CA	RYR	Texaco/Havoline	15	24	Ford
101.	06/17/90	Pocono, PA	RYR	Texaco/Havoline	12	5	Ford
102.	06/24/90	Brooklyn, MI	RYR	Texaco/Havoline	10	36	Ford
103.	07/07/90	Daytona Beach, FL	RYR	Texaco/Havoline	17	24	Ford
104.	07/22/90	Pocono, PA	RYR	Texaco/Havoline	15	5	Ford
105.	07/29/90	Talladega, AL	RYR	Texaco/Havoline	2	20	Ford
106.	08/12/90	Watkins Glen, NY	RYR	Texaco/Havoline	21	19	Ford
107.	08/19/90	Brooklyn, MI	RYR	Texaco/Havoline	10	6	Ford
108.	08/25/90	Bristol, TN	RYR	Texaco/Havoline	12	23	Ford
109.	09/02/90	Darlington, SC	RYR	Texaco/Havoline	12	15	Ford
110.	09/09/90	Richmond, VA	RYR	Texaco/Havoline	8	16	Ford
111.	09/16/90	Dover, DE	RYR	Texaco/Havoline	7	9	Ford
112.	09/23/90	Martinsville, VA	RYR	Texaco/Havoline	22	7	Ford
113.	09/30/90	No. Wilkesboro, NC	RYR	Texaco/Havoline	13	26	Ford
114.	10/07/90	Charlotte, NC	RYR	Texaco/Havoline	5	1	Ford
115.	10/22/90	Rockingham, NC	RYR	Texaco/Havoline	2	29	Ford
116.	11/04/90	Phoenix, AZ	RYR	Texaco/Havoline	4	11	Ford
117.	11/18/90	Atlanta, GA	RYR	Texaco/Havoline	4	25	Ford
118.	02/17/91	Daytona Beach, FL	RYR	Texaco/Havoline	1	15	Ford
119.	02/24/91	Richmond, VA	RYR	Texaco/Havoline	1	12	Ford
120.	03/03/91	Rockingham, NC	RYR	Texaco/Havoline	3	16	Ford
121.	03/17/91	Atlanta, GA	RYR	Texaco/Havoline	8	40	Ford
122.	04/07/91	Darlington, SC	RYR	Texaco/Havoline	11	2	Ford
123.	04/14/91	Bristol, TN	RYR	Texaco/Havoline	3	3	Ford
124.	04/21/91	No. Wilkesboro, NC	RYR	Texaco/Havoline	26	6	Ford
125.	04/28/91	Martinsville, VA	RYR	Texaco/Havoline	26	8	Ford
126.	05/06/91	Talladega, AL	RYR	Texaco/Havoline	4	22	Ford
127.	05/26/91	Charlotte, NC	RYR	Texaco/Havoline	10	1	Ford
128.	06/02/91	Dover, DE	RYR	Texaco/Havoline	11	16	Ford
129.	06/09/91	Sears Point, CA	RYR	Texaco/Havoline	13	1	Ford
130.	06/16/91	Pocono, PA	RYR	Texaco/Havoline	10	12	Ford
131.	06/23/91	Brooklyn, MI	RYR	Texaco/Havoline	4	1	Ford
132.	07/06/91	Daytona Beach, FL	RYR	Texaco/Havoline	2	3	Ford
133.	07/21/91	Pocono, PA	RYR	Texaco/Havoline	5	14	Ford
134.	07/28/91	Talladega, AL	RYR	Texaco/Havoline	7	9	Ford
135.	08/11/91	Watkins Glen, NY	RYR	Texaco/Havoline	9	10	Ford
136.	08/18/91	Brooklyn, MI	RYR	Texaco/Havoline	3	2	Ford
137.	08/24/91	Bristol, TN	RYR	Texaco/Havoline	7	24	Ford
138.	09/01/91	Darlington, SC	RYR	Texaco/Havoline	1	12	Ford
139.	09/07/91	Richmond, VA	RYR	Texaco/Havoline	3	2	Ford
140.	09/15/91	Dover, DE	RYR	Texaco/Havoline	2	31	Ford
141.	09/22/91	Martinsville, VA	RYR	Texaco/Havoline	25	29	Ford
142.	09/29/91	No. Wilkesboro, NC	RYR	Texaco/Havoline	2	4	Ford
143.	10/06/91	Charlotte, NC	RYR	Texaco/Havoline	2	2	Ford
144.	10/20/91	Rockingham, NC	RYR	Texaco/Havoline	10	1	Ford
145.	11/03/91	Phoenix, AZ	RYR	Texaco/Havoline	13	1	Ford
146.	11/17/91	Atlanta, GA	RYR	Texaco/Havoline	6	17	Ford
147.	02/16/92	Daytona Beach, FL	RYR	Texaco/Havoline	6	1	Ford
148.	03/01/92	Rockingham, NC	RYR	Texaco/Havoline	10	2	Ford
149.	03/08/92	Richmond, VA	RYR	Texaco/Havoline	2	4	Ford
150.	03/15/92	Atlanta, GA	RYR	Texaco/Havoline	25	4	Ford
151.	03/29/92	Darlington, SC	RYR	Texaco/Havoline	5	4	Ford
152.	04/05/92	Bristol, TN	RYR	Texaco/Havoline	6	28	Ford
153.	04/12/92	No. Wilkesboro, NC	RYR	Texaco/Havoline	7	1	Ford
154.	04/26/92	Martinsville, VA	RYR	Texaco/Havoline	23	26	Ford
155.	05/03/92	Talladega, AL	RYR	Texaco/Havoline	2	1	Ford
155A.	05/16/92	The Winston	RYR	Texaco/Havoline	1	1	Ford
156.	05/24/92	Charlotte, NC	RYR	Texaco/Havoline	17	4	Ford
157.	05/31/92	Dover, DE	RYR	Texaco/Havoline	21	11	Ford
158.	06/07/92	Sears Point, CA	RYR	Texaco/Havoline	10	28	Ford
159.	06/14/92	Pocono, PA	RYR	Texaco/Havoline	18	5	Ford
160.	06/21/92	Brooklyn, MI	RYR	Texaco/Havoline	1	1	Ford
161.	07/04/92	Daytona Beach, FL	RYR	Texaco/Havoline	3	10	Ford
162.	07/19/92	Pocono, PA	RYR	Texaco/Havoline	1	33	Ford
163.	07/26/92	Talladega, AL	RYR	Texaco/Havoline	3	3	Ford
164.	08/09/92	Watkins Glen, NY	RYR	Texaco/Havoline	11	20	Ford
165.	08/16/92	Brooklyn, MI	RYR	Texaco/Havoline	3	5	Ford
166.	08/29/92	Bristol, TN	RYR	Texaco/Havoline	7	30	Ford
167.	09/06/92	Darlington, SC	RYR	Texaco/Havoline	6	5	Ford
168.	09/12/92	Richmond, VA	RYR	Texaco/Havoline	5	19	Ford
169.	09/20/92	Dover, DE	RYR	Texaco/Havoline	29	4	Ford
170.	09/28/92	Martinsville, VA	RYR	Texaco/Havoline	22	16	Ford
171.	10/05/92	No. Wilkesboro, NC	RYR	Texaco/Havoline	14	11	Ford
172.	10/11/92	Charlotte, NC	RYR	Texaco/Havoline	22	20	Ford
173.	10/25/92	Rockingham, NC	RYR	Texaco/Havoline	15	10	Ford
174.	11/01/92	Phoenix, AZ	RYR	Texaco/Havoline	12	1	Ford
175.	11/15/92	Atlanta, GA	RYR	Texaco/Havoline	17	27	Ford
176.	02/13/93	Daytona Beach, FL	RYR	Texaco/Havoline	11	28	Ford
177.	02/28/93	Rockingham, NC	RYR	Texaco/Havoline	39	14	Ford
178.	03/07/93	Richmond, VA	RYR	Texaco/Havoline	14	1	Ford
179.	03/20/93	Atlanta, GA	RYR	Texaco/Havoline	31	13	Ford
180.	03/28/93	Darlington, SC	RYR	Texaco/Havoline	9	11	Ford
181.	04/04/93	Bristol, TN	RYR	Texaco/Havoline	10	5	Ford
182.	04/18/93	No. Wilkesboro, NC	RYR	Texaco/Havoline	27	4	Ford
183.	04/25/93	Martinsville, VA	RYR	Texaco/Havoline	6	2	Ford
184.	05/02/93	Talladega, AL	RYR	Texaco/Havoline	5	7	Ford
185.	05/16/93	Sears Point, CA	RYR	Texaco/Havoline	9	15	Ford
185A.	05/22/93	The Winston	RYR	Texaco/Havoline	5	9	Ford
186.	05/30/93	Charlotte, NC	RYR	Texaco/Havoline	23	30	Ford
187.	06/06/93	Dover, DE	RYR	Texaco/Havoline	3	3	Ford
188.	06/13/93	Pocono, PA	RYR	Texaco/Havoline	7	6	Ford
189.	06/20/93	Brooklyn, MI	RYR	Texaco/Havoline	3	35	Ford
190.	07/03/93	Daytona Beach, FL	RYR	Texaco/Havoline	3	31	Ford
191.	07/11/93	Loudon, NH	RYR	Texaco/Havoline	7	3	Ford

David Carl Allison
February 25, 1961 – July 13, 1993